AF614497

From A Grandfather's Heart

by

Granddad
(Robert Butler)

Published by Lulu.com

ISBN # 978-0-557-43383-4

DEDICATION

The idea for this book has been in my thoughts for quite some time. Actually, I wrote a series of letters to my grandson for his mother to give to him someday. Those "notes" were along the same lines as the counsel contained within this book. It wasn't then, nor is it now, my concern that I won't be around to provide grandfatherly words of wisdom to him and his sister. It is merely a precaution against the unknown nature of life and my personal fate. While I can't say that I've always lived by these ideas, I do believe that they would hold in good stead anyone who follows them. Others throughout history have said the same things, but I don't think that they can ever be repeated too often.

There may be those who will read this book and say that I am being very naïve, that people can't live this way. I think that it's cynical to say that our children shouldn't be taught to live as good people, with love in their hearts. With your eyes open to the wickedness around us, it isn't naïve to try to do the right thing. When we stop trying to be "good people," the world is doomed. I have to be optimistic and believe that we can make things better, one person at a time. That's what I want for my children, their children, and everyone else's children.

The world can be a difficult and oftentimes "wicked" place in which to live; following this set of "guidelines" could alleviate much of the world's pain and sadness. To that end, I offer the words that follow in the spirit of goodwill and hope that anyone who reads this and uses it makes the world around him/her a little better place to be.

I hereby dedicate this book to my grandchildren, who I love as much my own children.

Granddad

Note

Since it becomes a matter of opinion as to the order of importance of these "topics," they are in no particular order. The table of contents can be the reader's guide to the topic needed or of most interest at any given moment.

I have included a copy of the poem "Desiderata" at the end of this book because I believe that it presents a wondrous way of living life. I hope that you agree.

Table of Contents

Honesty

"If it's not yours, don't take it!" That seems like a very simple adage; however, the jails and prisons are filled with men and women who never heard those words, were never taught to respect other people's property, thought that, for some reason, they had a right to take something without paying for it, or just don't have a conscience (there are people who's brains are wired wrong). "Borrowing" without permission is just like stealing.

I remember taking a candy bar from a store when I was twelve years old. A friend of mine got me to do it (which is a terrible excuse, allowing someone else to make my decisions for me), but I couldn't eat it. I felt so guilty and was so scared that I'd get caught, that I took it back to the store and put it back on the shelf later that day. My friend never knew that; I was too "chicken" to admit it.

Guilt can be a powerful enemy, one with whom you do not want to do battle. It will eat at your very soul if you carry the weight of some theft with you, however small you might think it is. It won't ever leave you. I still feel guilty for having stolen that candy bar, as silly as it seems now at my age. That is only one of the instances in my life that have contributed to the "sack" of guilt or shame that I carry around with me. I can put it down from time to time and pretend that it's not there and that it doesn't bother me, but I can't go anywhere without that sack. It's mine forever.

The thing is, there is nothing that I can ever do to change what I did. The past can't be corrected. Even if I paid back $100 for every $1 for which I feel guilt, it wouldn't erase the fact that I "did the crime."

Sometimes it's a hard thing to live with, but I "made my bed, so I have to lie in it."

How important is being honest, trustworthy if you will? Think of it in these terms: would you want someone for a friend if you couldn't trust him or her? I hope not. If you were hiring people, would you hire someone who was a thief, because that's what a person who steals is, a thief!

Your reputation for honesty is an important part of your character. No one should ever be able to question your honesty.

My advice: keep your hands to yourself! If it's not yours, leave it where you find it!

Truth

"I cannot tell a lie; I chopped down the cherry tree," is the story that is supposedly attributed to George Washington as a boy. It's a good line to live by!

One of the things which my children were told repeatedly as they grew up was that they could tell us anything, anytime, and that we would believe them without hesitation; that is, until they lied to us and lost our trust in them. I like to use the analogy of having a "trust bank account." Every time you tell the truth, regardless of the consequences (and my kids never did anything that bad anyway), you are making a deposit to that account. It builds and builds over time, day by day. If one day, someone accuses you of something, I'm able to believe you, no doubt in my mind, because you have earned that trust through your deposits into the "trust account of truth." I will defend you and believe you because you earned it. Quite the opposite is true as well. If you've always told fibs and made yourself untrustworthy, then when something serious happens, I'll hesitate and have doubts. It's not a position in which you would want to find yourself.

Parents want to believe their children. They want to trust them. While punishment might be bad, it's better to suffer for something that you've done and keep people's trust in your word so that you won't suffer later if you are ever suspected or accused of something that you didn't do but can't prove it. It's very hard to disprove a negative.

Simply tell the truth. One lie can lead to another lie, which can lead to another lie. If you always tell the truth, you won't have to keep your stories straight. If there's only one version, the truth, then you'll always tell the same one.

"But what about lying to protect someone?" I was once asked. If you do that, you are as guilty as the person who you are protecting. You will be a better friend if you just tell the truth and stand by your friend through whatever the consequences. If you believe your friend to be innocent, work to find out the truth that will prove their innocence.

Of course, I'm not talking about telling a "white lie." If a girl asks if you think her hair looks nice, just say yes, you think so, or think of a nice way to say no. Avoiding hurting someone's feelings when it is something trivial is not a bad thing.

One last thing that I must mention is the Bible commandment, "Thou shalt not bear false witness." To me, this should not be confused with lying as I have discussed. Bearing false witness is claiming that someone is guilty of something when you know differently. That is, of course, WRONG! If you're ***always telling*** *ing* ***the truth****, you will never "bear false witness."*

Furthermore, if you don't know anything (or very little) about a matter being discussed, just sit quietly without commenting. Better to stay away from a subject rather than confuse the discussion even more with "guesses" or "rumors." If you don't care to spend the time learning the facts, then you have no business discussing it with people who may or may not know any more than you do. That's how "false information" gets spread until it seems to be truth, which is the same as telling lies.

A Kind Heart

"Do unto others as you would have them do unto you," is the Golden Rule and the only way to live. That's not to say that life will allow it to be that easy. It probably won't, but kindness to others is good for the heart. I find it difficult to believe that anyone likes being bullied or made fun of or taken advantage of or any of the many other ways that some kids (and adults too) seem to enjoy doing to those less fortunate or simply different for whatever reason. I refuse to believe that it is "human nature" for the stronger to prey on the weaker. I believe it has more to do with the environment in which a child is reared.

If parents tolerate or encourage children to be bullies or racists or simply inconsiderate to others, that's probably the way that the parents were raised. It is very similar to the "cycle of violence" that exists in abusive homes. Parents who treat their children and others with respect and kindness usually have children who demonstrate the same behaviors toward their peers.

Be friendly toward everyone, even those who treat you unkindly. Make friends with those who others shun because they are different. A few kind words from you could be their saving grace. All kids need friends, people who care about their feelings. Until you have a reason to avoid someone, don't. There is good in everyone, though it is more difficult to find in a few.

There is an old saying which is very true. "If you don't have something good to say, don't say anything." Better to just smile and be silent than to say something which could hurt someone's feelings. It will only add to your "shame sack" of guilt. If your brain malfunctions for a moment and you do utter a few unkind words, apologize quickly. Never *let bad feelings or thoughts linger in your head. It's like a bad apple; it will rot slowly and infect other things.*

Compassion

Having an awareness of the distress of another and the desire to relieve it is being compassionate. This is one of the greatest characteristics of a good person, something which I hope that my grandkids strive to achieve. I can't say that I've always acted on my feelings of compassion, but I would like to think that I would have if I'd been able.

At an early age, I lived in Venezuela and Colombia during the late 1950's and early 60's. As an American family, our standard of living far exceeded most of the people around us. I witnessed abject poverty and wondered why it had to exist. There was nothing that I could have done as a child, but I felt that something wasn't right. No one should live that way. Children walked the streets with only a pair of shorts, most with no shoes. Some of the areas (slums, I suppose) were nothing but lean-to's or shanty-type huts. There was no indoor plumbing in these areas. Raw sewage ran in the gutters of the streets so far as I could tell. While I didn't walk through these areas, we did pass them whenever we left home to go somewhere. It was terrible.

While that is not the norm in the United States, there are still many people who will grow up with fewer advantages in life than your parents can provide for you. As I write this, I am spending a year in Iowa as a VISTA member (Volunteers in Service to America). I chose to do this because I've long felt the need to give back for the blessings that I've enjoyed my whole life. I hope that you will take the opportunity to volunteer whenever an appropriate venue comes your way. It should be a part of your life to help others who, for whatever reason, find themselves in need of assistance.

This world can be a cruel and heartless place. Decisions that we make can either help or hurt others. Try to make yours with compassion in your heart. It's one of the things which make us human.

Generosity

Give some of what you have so that others will have enough, whether it is for clothes, food, shelter, medical care, education, or whatever. I have always said that if I won millions of dollars that there would be lots of happy people out there. In my heart, I know that I couldn't do what I've seen so many other people do, live like someone privileged while others struggle to get ahead in life. Sure, I'd keep enough to have a home, a car, and enough so that I wouldn't do without, but the rest would be divided among family and friends as I feel appropriate. If I then had any left, it would be used to fund charitable needs close to my heart: a food bank, Goodwill and Salvation Army clothing stores, tutoring/training centers for people who need help improving their lot in life, and free clinics so that no one would have to go without seeing a doctor or dentist because of a lack of money. For me, there are certain human rights which exist in life: food, shelter, clothing, education, and medical care. No one should have to do without these: according to their needs!

Be generous not only with money but your time as well. That is the most precious gift that you can give. You gain when you spend time talking to someone who is suffering or when you tutor a fellow classmate who is struggling with a class. There is no other feeling like the one that you get when someone succeeds or survives because of your efforts. Even if you don't get a "thank you," your heart will feel good. It's a selfishly wonderful feeling to know that another person is better off for having had you in his life. Teachers know this feeling better than most other people. Students often forget to say "thanks," but a smile works just the same. Be generous with both.

Give whenever you can. It's a great feeling!

Tolerance

Throughout your life, you will encounter many people who are different from you. Whether it is the culture in which they are raised or the religious beliefs that they have or the color of their skin or the unusual accent with which they speak, accept others just as you would expect them to accept you for your differences. Tolerance is crucial to peace between people.

If you have spent time learning about how people in different countries live, what they eat, their history, their cultures, and the many other facets of their lives, then you will understand why they think and act the way that they do. It is usually the unknowns that make us fear them.

Be open to listening to other points of view, though you may reject them once you have heard them. It is when people think that they are not being heard that potential problems arise. Be understanding and open to views other than those which you hold. Rumors and outright lies cause heartache and pain. "Believe nothing of what you hear and only half of what you see," may be a bit harsh, but it comes close to being good advice. Beware of making quick judgments, especially about those who have been raised in a different environment from yours. Being different doesn't make them wrong and you right. Take the time to learn about people before you dismiss them or their concerns about life or the world.

There is one area of life which has lead to more death and strife in this world than any other: religious dogma (and the misunderstanding of the same). Religious beliefs are very personal things for most people. While most leaders of the world's leading religions teach tolerance and encourage understanding and cooperation among organizations, there are those sects and individuals who take radical positions from which they believe that they are entitled to commit crimes. These small groups and individuals are the problem, not the semantic or rite differences between the religious beliefs. Avoid these groups like you would a diseased rat! People are people and generally just want to live in peace and to follow their personal beliefs. My philosophy is that "people have a right to do or believe anything so long as it doesn't impinge on my personal beliefs or actions." While I might disagree with others, so long as their beliefs don't prevent me from living a free and happy life, then they can believe whatever they want.

Again, learn about the teachings of other religions. Read the Qur'an (Quran, Qur'ān, Koran, Al-Coran or Al-Qur'ān), the sacred texts of Buddhism, and the Torah, not just the Bible (whichever of the versions with which you have been "indoctrinated"). (One note: be careful of English translations of religious books. Translations can make all the difference in the world.) Knowledge leads to understanding and wisdom. Do you really think that God would want you to hate someone else and do violence in his name? I hope not. There are parts of all religions which are the same. The practical application and rites might be very different, but the basic tenets are the same: the sanctity of life and the belief in a power greater than us. No one knows for certain what the truth is. We can only believe and have faith. Christians may be wrong. Muslims may be wrong. Jews may be wrong. Buddhists may be wrong. No one will know until after death, if even then. All that anyone can do is live according to the golden rule and let others live in peace.

Keeping the Faith...

I have never been and probably never will be a "church" person. It's not that I don't think that's a good thing, but it's just not me. If going to church gives you comfort and helps you have peace of mind, then go. Religion, organized religion, has never held much interest for me, but it can be a powerful force for good, and, unfortunately, for bad too. I look at it this way: if your church or religion or faith (whatever you call it) encourages the ideals of compassion, kindness, love, tolerance (of other people and other religions), understanding of others, and non-violence, then I say that's a good thing. If it makes you a better person, then it's a good thing. If, however, it doesn't, either there's something wrong with the religion (or particular church, synagogue, temple, mosque, etc. which you attend) or the messenger (minister, pastor, priest, whatever). Walk, no, **run** *away from it to one which supports "love thy neighbor." There's too much hate and distrust in the world now; don't become a part of the problem.*

*One of the things which I've seen since while being in Iowa with AmeriCorps*VISTA are churches which spend much of their time helping people in need.* ***THAT****, in my opinion, is what churches should be about, not trying to raise money to build bigger churches and provide big salaries and easy living to ministers or evangelists or whoever. If it weren't for the churches (all denominations) in Cedar Rapids, the flood recovery would have taken years longer, and people would have suffered more. Whether it has been raising money to purchase building materials, feeding volunteers and victims, housing them, operating food banks, or whatever else was needed, the churches here did it (and are still doing it). That's what I think churches should be doing, why they should exist.*

It's not about teaching Sunday school classes and having a church service once or twice a week. It should be "doing God's work!"

Whether you choose to follow the beliefs that your parents teach you or not, that is something which you will have to decide. Whether you choose to be called a Christian or Muslim or Buddhist or Jew or anything else, it makes no difference to me. Believe whatever gives you peace of mind and a good heart for people. Learn about other religions so that you understand how other people worship and appreciate the gift of life that we have. Always remember that each religion has its own group of fanatics who distort the teachings of its faith. Don't let those fanatics persuade you to hate or distrust groups of people as a whole. Make up your own mind based on personal research and understanding of other faiths. Always remember: **NO ONE KNOWS FOR CERTAIN WHAT THE REAL TRUTH IS ABOUT GOD OR THE MEANING OF LIFE.** *It boils down to a matter of* **FAITH!**

Speaking of faith, I don't just mean "faith in God;" I mean faith in yourself and your abilities. Have faith in yourself, in your intelligence, in your determination to do right, and in your ability to overcome hardship. You won't always win or succeed; nobody does all the time. However, optimism is having faith that in the end, good things will come to you because you work hard and do things the right way. I have faith in you, as do your parents.

"...To thine own self be true..."

By the time you read Hamlet, by William Shakespeare, you'll be ready to understand what this chapter title means. You will have matured to the point where you can begin to see what is important to you as a person. Your guiding principles will, for the most part, be ingrained in your heart and soul. Hopefully they will include most, if not all, of the precepts which are included in this "book." It is to those principles that you must remain true and loyal, if at all possible.

Of course, I could conjure up various scenarios where you might be forced to violate your core principles for the sake of someone's life, but those events happen rarely for any person. This discussion is about the day-to-day activities and decisions which you will make as you interact with people and the world around you. If, as an example, someone badgers you about being understanding and tolerant of a person "outside" of your group of friends, speak up and defend either your right to your own opinion or why you don't condemn the person in question. I sincerely hope that you don't remain silent as others taunt or ridicule someone or, worse, join with them against your better nature. That is remaining true to yourself. Until you've "walked a mile" in another person's shoes, so-to-speak, you really shouldn't be judging him. I know that there are exceptions to this rule and that it is sometimes hard to buck popular opinion, but following the crowd can be a dangerous and shameful path to walk.

Even more difficult challenges will present themselves as you get older, especially in the workplace, wherever that might be for you. Still, speaking truthfully and honestly, so long as you do it in a respectful and positive way, will do more for how you are perceived by those around you than keeping silent in the face of racism or discrimination or bullying. If you stand by and say nothing, then you are passively endorsing whatever is being said or inadvertently encouraging the behavior that you believe in your heart to be wrong. Should any harm come to someone because of your silent consent, you will feel terribly guilty. In some extreme situations, you could actually be saving a life through your positive speech or actions.

I know that these things are often very difficult to do. I have looked the other way at times, which I'm certain you will as well. That doesn't change the fact that I was wrong or that you will be wrong. It is for the strong to defend the weak. It is for all of us to withhold our opinion (judgment, if you will) until all of the facts are known. Just as important is for you to "stay out of other people's business" unless it involves defending someone who cannot defend himself. Now, if that means physical danger, the first reaction should be to notify the police, not put yourself in harm's way unless you have no choice. That's a decision that only you can make at the time. Be careful and certain of your actions before you risk your life. The only time that such rash action is understandable is when family or close friends' lives are in danger.

There may come a time in your life when you are asked to "bend the truth" or "not say anything" in a business or professional situation. My only advice is to do what your heart tells you is the right thing. I know that paying bills and supporting a family can often present a terrible choice at those moments. If you bend to the will of your boss, then you should begin to search for another job and leave as soon as you secure one. Compromising your principles is not worth it. Should the problem involve your being asked to lie or breaking the law, there should be no question about what you will do. Say no and then find another job! You don't want to work for a company that operates that way.

Again, the world can be a wicked and deceitful place, but you can make it better by sticking to your principles. When others know that you stand for what is right, they will respect and admire you. That's more important than any job or any amount of money.

Forever a Student

If you ever think that you know it all, you have a problem. Life is an ever-changing, circular stage upon which we all must adapt and grow. Consider the lifespan of the "lily of the valley." It is a perennial flowering plant which can live many years, producing flowers each season. So long as it adapts to the growing conditions each year, it thrives and blooms, spreading its beauty and wonder among the other plants around it. However, if it stops adapting or suffers from disease which it cannot fight off, it will die, much like a human being. So too much each of us learn and grow and adapt as the world around us changes. If we don't adapt, we soon become isolated and suffer, eventually dying. Yes, all humans eventually die anyway, but you can expect a long, happy, fruitful life if you continue to learn, maintain that curiosity which is the human spirit and take care of the only body which you will ever have.

From the time that you are born, you are watching and learning, absorbing the subtleties of the world and the people around you. Your parents are your most important teachers. As you grow older, you will attend school, either public or private, or be home-schooled (at least until your parents can no longer properly educate you). Eventually, I hope, you will go to college (or some formal training facility), a place where you will be thrown into a world which is a collage of ideas, many of which may be completely foreign to you. Seek out and learn as much as you can, adding the good ones to your mental library and rejecting those which your heart tells you are either wrong for you or dangerous. It's not always an easy task, but it's one that we all must complete. Learn all that you can, whether your life's choice is to be a teacher or a doctor or a plumber or whatever else suits you. You won't learn everything in school; the "real world" of work and struggle and life itself will continue to teach you things that aren't taught in schools.

If you choose to marry, then you'll learn from your wife, just as she will learn from you. For two people to successfully share life, there must be communication and learning. It is the hardest job that you will ever have, being someone else's "partner for life." Not everyone can do it.

If and when you have children, you will primarily be the teacher until they outgrow your knowledge base and then begin to teach you. I have learned much from my children and continue to do so, even though at times it is hard. (I'm still not a texting person and probably never will be.)

The point is that when you stop learning and sit back in that easy chair, you have begun to die. The rest of your life is little more than waiting for that moment when you will close your eyes for the last time and drift off to permanent sleep. I agree with Dylan Thomas, who wrote, "Rage, rage against the dying of the light!" The only way to do that is to keep learning, keep adapting to your body's changes and the world around you. So long as you are healthy and have family and friends around whom love you, this life is worth living. Besides, no one really knows what lies on the other side of consciousness. Don't be in a hurry to find out.

Hard Work Pays Off!

There are those who might argue the opposite is true, and sometimes it seems that way. However, don't believe anyone who says otherwise; this life gives you little that you don't earn. Opportunities will come your way when others see how determined and dedicated you are to whatever craft you choose.

Now, I'm not advising you to be a "workaholic," more focused on work than on your personal life. What I'm saying is that if you study and practice and learn whatever there is to know about your chosen field, good things will happen for you. There are only a handful of truly "gifted" people in the world at any given time that possess an innate ability which allows them to excel without hard work. However, even they cannot reach their full potentials unless they focus on what is important.

The greatest athletes, musicians, singers, actors, scientists, or whoever are those who practice, learn from others, ask hard questions of themselves and their peers, never stop learning about their craft and what it takes to be at their best. If you want to be a champion swimmer, you must swim miles and miles while building your body and endurance. You would learn techniques which make you turn faster at the wall and develop efficient strokes so that you expend less energy while expelling the greatest thrust in the water. That's what a champion does.

The same thing is true of a doctor. The time spent in medical school is invaluable if used wisely. Study, learn from books, ask questions of those who have the experience and knowledge that you need, and practice the skills that should become second nature to a doctor. An experienced nurse has much to offer a doctor-in-training, so ego has to be put aside so that learning can take place. Never be afraid to ask questions of someone who has answers. The goal is to develop your brain and hands and heart so that one day you'll have the skills necessary to help someone in need.

No one ever learns everything; the world, and its knowledge base, is expanding daily. If you ever think that you have learned it all or know enough, then it might be time to retire. Surely there are new questions to be asked, new mountains to be climbed, other people to be helped.

One thing though, you should take time to relax every day. Whether it's a five minute walk alone outside in the fresh air away from the pressures of life or simply sitting back in a chair and closing your eyes while taking a few deep breaths, it's important for your heart and your mind to escape to "nothingness" for a brief interlude. Create two lives: one at work or school and another away from them with loved ones where you refocus on what's equally important in your life: love and home.

LOVE...So Very Important!

A life without love is a life unlived. It is the lifeblood of living. Not everyone is lucky enough to find a "soul mate," but it happens more than people admit. It might take some time, but be aware that it can be "just around the corner." That's not the only kind of love in this world.

Many things can be important in your life: work, hobbies, or a favorite sporting team. However, those can't provide you with the gift of love. People are what really count in this life. The sacrifice that one makes for another is love. Whether it's a soldier stepping in front of a bullet to save a comrade's life or a little girl giving her favorite doll to another girl who doesn't have one, that's love. Helping a fellow student, whether a close friend or just someone in class, that's love. Working an extra hour so that another worker can go home and study for tomorrow's test, even though you are tired and hungry, that's love. Putting your last fifty cents into that charity jar at the convenience store to help a family who was the victim of a fire, even though you had planned to put it in your own jar at home to save for a new video game, that's love.

There is a natural love which exists between members of a family; for most people it comes with their DNA. Unfortunately, some have more than others, and some struggle to express it, even though it's there, deep inside their heart. Never be afraid to tell those who you love how you feel. "Tomorrow is promised to no one," so make sure that your feelings are known. I didn't grow up in a family that hugged or said "I love you" very often. It was only when I married into a family that did and had my own children that I learned to be more open with my feelings, though some would say that's not the case. My children changed me in so many ways. Today, I can't imagine my life without them.

One of the most difficult kinds of love to understand and express is teenage love. When you face those feelings for the first time, you need to be careful about using those three little words. "I love you" can mean different things to different people. If you feel the need to use those words with someone for whom you have deep feelings (at that young age), it would be advisable to explain what you mean by it. Chances are that your feelings of love aren't the "lifelong, everlasting" kind, though a few couples do find a soul mate at a young age. Be cautious; choose your words carefully; take it slowly; and let the mutual feelings grow between you. Too much "love" can be like "too much sugar," bad for your health (mental as well as physical). Use it sparingly. It will last longer and be more enjoyable for both of you. Young love is fragile; it breaks easily and hurts deeply.

Friendship is another kind of love, one which requires loyalty and trust and, quite often, forgiveness when a friend breaks a promise. A friend will be a cheerleader, a counselor, a supporter, a sounding board, and even a bit of conscience when the situation calls for it. Only someone who loves you is truly your friend, and vice versa. A friend protects a friend from others from the "slings and arrows" of others as well as from himself (example: friends don't let friends do drugs or drive after drinking).

Romantic love is the purest form of self-love. Giving yourself to another in whatever form that may take is the only way to receive love. It cannot be a one-way street; that's not truly love. If the person who you love doesn't feel the same way, cannot express love to you in the manner that you can, then grieve for what might have been and continue your search. With time and patience, love will find you. When it does arrive, it will have been worth the wait.

Appreciate the Gift

There's one more thing about school: as you grow up and move from elementary to high school to college and beyond, keep one thought in mind. School is your job. Your parents work and take care of you so that you can have the time and freedom to learn and grow into an adult, one who will be able to pursue whatever goals that you might have. That is quite a gift, one that not every child is given. You have an obligation to do your very best to learn in and out of class, to allow others to do the same without disruption or distraction by you, and to do nothing to dishonor or embarrass yourself or your family. That doesn't mean that you are expected to make all A's in school; it means that you will have given your best effort. Remember that not all teens (or even younger children) have the luxury of concentrating on learning without distractions such as part-time jobs or caring for a house or younger siblings because of needs at home.

Appreciate the sacrifices and hard work that your parents and others in your life have made for you. You will do the same thing when your turn comes. Peace, a full stomach, a gentle hand on your shoulder when you're in pain, moral and physical support when you need it, and so many other things don't just happen. They are the conscious decisions by those who love you!

Take the time to say "Thank you" and "I love you" to all of those people who do kindnesses or sacrifice for you. That, and your hard work, is all that they ask in return.

Money

First, money is not the "root of all evil," nor is "the love of money the root of all evil." Money is merely a means to an end, that end being whatever you need or want in life. Having said that, I must warn you that money and the accumulation of the same can become a terrible addiction. Sure, we all need money to pay the bills and get those things which we choose to believe are important. However, family and friends should be more important than the gathering of wealth.

It's funny. I have a degree in business with a major in accounting, but Grandma Kay is probably a better person from whom to obtain counsel when it comes to matters of money. I haven't done too good a job managing it over the years. It has given me a position from which to give a bit of advice though, at least concerning a few things.

First, avoid credit cards of all types. They are money pits, designed by those who have money to drain the rest of us of ours. Interest charges and that deceptive "minimum payment" have been the downfall of millions of people. Here in 2010 (as I write this), it appears that those interest charges and other unscrupulous fees will only be going higher while the credit card companies shrink credit lines, even for those who have never had a problem with paying their credit card bills. Therefore, it is best if you avoid them, period! My advice is that if you don't have the cash, don't buy it. Of course that doesn't apply to large purchases such as a home or car. Credit will always be necessary for these investments.

Second, don't lend people money, period! The quickest way to ruin friendship is to lend money. If you have it, and they really need it, just give it to them. Hopefully they will repay it someday, but you should give it without expecting it to be returned. If you do that, then at least you can remain friends even if they can't because they feel guilty for taking it and then being unable to repay it. I know how hard it is to say no to friends, and I have borrowed from friends. I did pay them back, though once it took me three years to do it. Just remember, if you have to borrow from a friend, ALWAYS PAY IT BACK AS SOON AS YOU CAN!

There's an old saying that you should "pay yourself first." I agree. Start a savings account and save at least 10% whenever you are paid for work or are given some by relatives for birthdays or just as a gift for no particular reason. Don't touch that money except to invest it wisely, as counseled (Grandma Kay again or someone else for whom you have great financial respect). Watch for savings programs which match your funds if you save for something like a car, a house, an education, or a business. Those can help you build a nest egg for specific purposes. Of course, NEVER have just one investment or one savings account. "Never put all your eggs (money) into one basket," the saying goes. That way, if you lose one basket, you will still have others. It does happen: investments sometimes "evaporate." If you recognize that now and plan for it, the pain will be less.

One other thing about money is that if you find yourself with more than you can possibly spend or need for your lifetime, give some to those who need it. Of course, I expect that you'll be generous with others and automatically think of that. Share your good fortune. Not everyone will have been as fortunate. Spread the wealth!

Be a Peaceful Soul

One of the things in my life about which I am most proud is that I have never hit another person, never been a man of violence. That's not to say that I haven't had feelings or thoughts along that line. I simply have never been in a physical fight with anyone, ever. I have come close a couple of times, but I always chose to walk away before words went too far. That doesn't mean that I'm a saint or that someone who has been in a fight is not a good person.

I believe that there are circumstances under which I would fight. I would defend to the death a family member, probably even a dear friend. I have always felt that I would do whatever it took to protect my children, any child for that matter. I've just never been in that position. I hope that I never am.

You may be faced with a bully or a situation where you are challenged to a fight. If you have done something to offend someone to the point where they want to fight, you should apologize and walk away, thereby defusing the situation. If you are threatened, go to whatever authority there is and report the threat. The only time that you should be in a fight is if you are attacked without provocation. Then, defend yourself; fight hard and fast until the attacker stops. Violence should be your last choice. If at all possible, walk away. Words might hurt, but it's better than one of you being severely injured, crippled, or worse.

Again, I have never had to fight. I have always used words and my wits to avoid fighting. Have I been called a coward or "chicken?" Yes, I have. However, my friends knew that walking away took more courage than rolling around in the dirt or being "punched out." There are *other solutions; at least there have been for me. I hope that is the case for you.*

One more thing—do whatever you can to prevent violence. Be a peacemaker whenever it is safe to do so. If you see two guys with weapons about to go at it, turn around and quickly go get help. If you see an argument that could get out of hand, offer your help to mediate the dispute before things get out of control. Use your "common sense" to decide when to get involved and when to go get help. Stay safe and help others do the same.

Final Thoughts…

While I have attempted to cover as much ground as possible, I'm sure that there's more that I would like to pass along. However, I know that my grandkids have wonderful parents to whom they will turn whenever they need counsel, which is as it should be. I trust that they will be as supportive of their children as I would like to think that their parents were of them. There will be times when growing pains and the natural rebellion of youth will create difficulties for both parties, but with patience, understanding, and the willingness to compromise (when compromise is an alternative), they will grow to be happy, healthy, productive adults.

May God bless them and all of us.

Desiderata

-- written by Max Ehrmann in the 1920s --

Go placidly amid the noise and the haste,
and remember what peace there may be in silence.

As far as possible, without surrender,
be on good terms with all persons.
Speak your truth quietly and clearly;
and listen to others,
even to the dull and the ignorant;
they too have their story.
Avoid loud and aggressive persons;
they are vexatious to the spirit.

If you compare yourself with others,
you may become vain or bitter,
for always there will be greater and lesser persons than yourself.
Enjoy your achievements as well as your plans.
Keep interested in your own career, however humble;
it is a real possession in the changing fortunes of time.

Exercise caution in your business affairs,
for the world is full of trickery.
But let this not blind you to what virtue there is;
many persons strive for high ideals,
and everywhere life is full of heroism.
Be yourself. Especially do not feign affection.
Neither be cynical about love,
for in the face of all aridity and disenchantment,
it is as perennial as the grass.

Take kindly the counsel of the years,
gracefully surrendering the things of youth.

Nurture strength of spirit to shield you in sudden misfortune.
But do not distress yourself with dark imaginings.
Many fears are born of fatigue and loneliness.

Beyond a wholesome discipline,
be gentle with yourself.
You are a child of the universe
no less than the trees and the stars;
you have a right to be here.
And whether or not it is clear to you,
no doubt the universe is unfolding as it should.

Therefore be at peace with God,
whatever you conceive Him to be.
And whatever your labors and aspirations,
in the noisy confusion of life,
keep peace in your soul.

With all its sham, drudgery, and broken dreams,
it is still a beautiful world.
Be cheerful. Strive to be happy.

HTTP://WWW.FLEURDELIS.COM/DESIDERATA.HTM

Other books by Robert Butler:

CHRISTIN

THE CHRISTMAS FAREWELL

2011 A GREAT ADVENTURE?
BOOK I IN THE SERIES

2012 A NEW BEGINNING?
BOOK II IN THE SERIES

2012 THE JOURNEY CONTINUES
BOOK III IN THE SERIES

2012 NEW HORIZON
BOOK IV IN THE SERIES

NO THOUGHT BUT TO LIVE
(FIRST FOUR BOOKS OF THE SERIES IN ONE VOLUME)

THE JOURNEY HOME

THE SUPPORT GROUP

Short Stories by GEORGE

Essay Writing Made Easier

All books are available at the following site:

http://stores.lulu.com/robertbutler

About the Author

*Robert Butler spent twelve years as a high school English teacher but has had several "careers," including six years as an accountant (his college diploma was in business, majoring in accounting), six years as a night security officer in Memphis, TN, a food service manager in both fast food and college food services, and a variety of odd jobs, one of which took him to Granby, Colorado for five months to work in conference services at Snow Mountain Ranch, the YMCA of the Rockies. He spent a year in Cedar Rapids, Iowa while a member of AmeriCorps*VISTA helping with the flood recovery work there. As of now, he could be anywhere, doing most anything, but he will be writing something.*

RGBUTLER62451@YAHOO.COM